Muir Woods

Redwood Refuge

by

JOHN HART

Contents

The Golden Gate National Park Association is a non-profit membership organization established to support the education, conservation and research programs of the Golden Gate National Recreation Area.

PUBLISHED BY
GOLDEN GATE NATIONAL
PARK ASSOCIATION

ISBN 0-9625206-4-0

It may be the most-looked-at ancient forest in the world. In long plain lines the redwoods rise, toward wind noise, or toward silence. They rise clear out of the place you walk in, the one made green and ferny by their shade. With their enormous height —few of the tops can really be seen—the massive red-brown boles seem almost spindly. Around their bases the visitors flock, and angle their necks to see, and click their cameras, and ask and answer.

Die Muir-Wälder. Muir Woods National Monument. Le Monument National de Muir Woods: brochures tell the story in four alphabets, eight languages; there is demand for as many more. Listen a few minutes in the parking lot on Saturday, and you'll hear a good number of them.

One of the first parks ever set aside for the coast redwood, named for a great and talkative conservationist who had little to do with its saving, Muir Woods now is an emblem. It represents the redwoods in a way in which other and greater redwood parks, on other and greater redwood-bordered streams farther away from the city, do not. For multitudes over the decades, these redwoods, so close to San Francisco and a stop on numerous tours, have been <u>the</u> redwoods: perhaps the only ones they will ever see.

Yet it is possible to walk through Muir Woods quickly, and take in rather little, to come away with nothing but a vague sense of coolness and postcard grandeur. That's inevitable, even appropriate. This is a place where nothing happens fast. In a forest of Sequoia sempervirens, time itself is the amazement; slowness, the very marvel.

"Very deep," writes Thomas Mann, "is the well of the past." There are few places where we see so far into that well as in a grove of coast redwoods—if we are able to take the time to look.

The rainy season at Muir Woods generally runs from mid-November to mid-April, with January the rainiest month (snow is a rarity). Coastal fog is common between early May and mid-September. The fog, drawn in by heat in interior valleys, tends to run in cycles, with a clear spell every few days.

The scientific name of the coast redwood is Sequoia sempervirens. The second word, often mistranslated 'everliving,' actually means 'evergreen.' The first half is based on the name of the Cherokee chief Sequoyah. The linkage may not be so far-fetched: Sequoyah gave his people an alphabet, and an alphabet, like a redwood tree, is something that endures.

§

Redwood Time: The Well of the Past

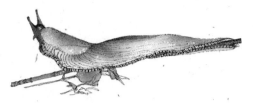

JUST INTO MUIR WOODS a mounted exhibit tells time, redwood-fashion. It is a cross-section of a tree just over a thousand years old. Until 1988, a cheerfully Anglocentric display picked out annual growth rings corresponding to the Battle of Hastings, the Magna Carta. Now we have New World events, from the founding of Mesa Verde to Columbus and beyond, encompassed in the lifetime of one tree.

We're meant to marvel at that thousand years, and do. But neither the Magna Carta nor Mesa Verde is anything but the very latest news—on the redwood scale of years.

Unlike the higher animals, unlike many other plants, redwoods apparently do not suffer physiological aging. They change as they get older, their growth slows down, but there is no inevitable deterioration. 'Immortal' is too big a word, yet this huge fact remains: there is no built-in reason why any particular redwood tree need ever die.

A look through the plant world shows that this open-ended life is not unique. The Douglas-firs that grow here and there in Muir Woods National Monument, for instance, likewise have no fixed lifespan. But very few other trees are as good as a redwood at defending themselves against natural enemies that limit potential lives. A Douglas-fir will lose a branch in a high wind; a fungus invades at the break; the end begins. A redwood with a broken limb or even a snapped-off crown is no more mortally ill than a human being with a broken arm.

There are a few redwood-eaters—a fungus or two that can colonize parts of a tree; a beetle or two that can pierce to the sapwood. But none of these do serious damage. Something about the wood—perhaps the particular form of tannin it contains, though the matter is poorly understood—resists invaders. Ecologist Stephen Veirs writes simply: "No killing diseases are known for established trees."

No killing diseases. Those short-lived, two-legged, rather noisy creatures down there among the ferns and huckleberry bushes—large-brained enough to look up and wonder: smart enough, too, to know what a lifespan is—can think about that for a moment, if they choose.

Of course, accidents, chiefly involving wind and fire, do occur. They happen frequently enough to limit the lifespan of the trees, in a practical sense. Time runs out for a redwood, too. But it is not Time itself that does the harm.

Burls and Sprouts

Going by ring-counts, even the coast redwood is not the longest-lived plant species known. Its cousin the giant sequoia, *Sequoiadendron giganteum*, a native of the Sierra Nevada range, reaches 3,000 years; the bristlecone pine of the White Mountains and other Great Basin mountaintops approaches 5,000.

But tree rings may not contain the whole story. Redwoods have two ways of reproducing. Some new trees begin with the seeds that fall by the bucketful, in fall and early winter, from insignificant-appearing cones. But just as often, a new trunk begins as a sprout from the base of an old one.

Almost from the moment it breaks out of the seed, a redwood seedling begins building what is called a burl ring. This is a dense mass of living shoots whose growth is begun but, for the moment, suppressed. As the tree establishes itself, the burl ring sinks into the soil. As the trunk expands, the ring widens with it and forms a heavy sheath both above and below the ground. But the upward growth of the incipient sprouts continues to be curbed, perhaps by a chemical signal biologists haven't yet identified.

If the parent tree gets into trouble, the natural brake is released. Sprouts from the burl ring explode toward the light. All at once, around the base of the stricken trunk, a ring of new shoots appears.

These burl-ring sprouts have a great advantage over plants beginning from seed: even when millimeters thick themselves, they have the root system of a mighty tree to feed them. They can take years, if necessary, to struggle up into the forest canopy, and they do.

And so arises the characteristic phenomenon of the sprout ring: circles of great trees surrounding an older tree, or a stump, or a vacancy. These rings are sometimes called 'family circles.' But the trees of the circle are not separate individuals, genetically related: they are a single individual, connected at the root, thrust up from the burl ring of a single ancient stem whose root is still alive.

How old is a redwood in a circle? Is it only as old as the annual rings in its bole? Or is it as old as the parent tree it derives from? And if age is measured by the root, just how old might such a redwood be?

There are precedents. Creosote bushes, growing in red-wood-like rings in the Mojave Desert, are thought to have common roots six or seven thousand years old. Some groups of aspens—which likewise are multi-stemmed trees, not stands of separate individuals—

Redwood Sprouts
A fully developed sprout ring stands within sight of the Muir Woods Visitor Center, about one hundred yards up the the main trail. And almost anywhere you look in the park, you'll see little hedges of sprouts at the base of standing redwoods: these, the Park Service says, are the result of trampling near the trees by generations of visitors. Particularly in earlier decades, when use was less controlled, traffic around the trunks compressed and eroded the soil enough to stress the trees and trigger this reproductive mechanism.

may be 8,000 years old at the root. Living coast redwood roots may reach ages as great as either creosote bushes or aspens—or greater. Somewhere, unidentified, possibly even in Muir Woods, there may grow a redwood that is the oldest living woody plant in the world.

Unchanged Through Time

But the well of the past suggested by that round slab of cut redwood is far deeper than the life of any individual tree, however you count it.

Perhaps because it reproduces so much by sprout, without the reshuffling of genes that goes with sexual reproduction, the redwood stands out among plants as an astonishing and—in its current, restricted range—triumphant conservative. In a changing world, as mountains rise and fall, as continents shift and jostle, the redwoods have changed rather little. Not for a very long time.

Redwoods not basically different from those at Muir Woods appear in the fossil record some 160 or 170 million years ago, in the period called the Jurassic—dinosaur days. Fossils are found across the Northern Hemisphere, in Manchuria and France, in Alaska and Greenland, even on the Arctic island Spitzbergen. A living relative, the *Metasequoia*, occurs in China. During most of the redwoods' career, all of these places (geologists believe) were parts of a single gigantic northern continent, Laurasia. At least the northern tier of Laurasia, it seems, was redwood country.

Muir Woods is as good a place as any to begin imagining that ancient world. You can start with the famous trees, and leave them much as they are. The sword ferns that grow at your feet are all right, too: if not this species, something rather like it would have grown in the old forest. The moss and mushrooms can stay. But you have to take away these California laurels, elongating toward the light. The big-leaf maples, too, must go: the Jurassic had not invented tall things with leaves. In their place in the understory are perhaps tree ferns, and gigantic versions of the little wiry horsetails that grow along the path.

Horsetail

That was then. The slow brute dance of the continents and oceanic plates has since shaped us a more rugged, less temperate world than the one in which the redwoods developed. The ancestors of today's coast redwoods did not evolve to meet these challenges. They merely retreated, and retreated, until today they occupy only this coastal strip, never more than thirty miles deep and about five hundred long, on the far western edge of the westernmost fragment of old Laurasia, what we know as North America.

It's always a stretch to imagine geologic time, to conceive of the planet's solid surfaces as bustling and fluid. It jolts the awareness again to encounter living forms that have outlasted not only their live contemporaries but even the basic continental shapes they evolved with. The redwoods are not the only such—the salmon in the creek that flows among them are also of a notably ancient strain, and the horsetails beside it go back farther even than do the trees above—but it would be hard to imagine survivors more dramatic than these high red forms.

John Muir, responding in 1908 to the news that Muir Woods was to be named for him, went straight to the point:

A Sierra peak also and one of the Alaska glaciers bear my name, but these aboriginal woods, barring human action, will outlast them all. Since the first Sequoia forests lifted their domes and spires to the sky, mountains great and small, thousands of them, have been weathered, ground away and cast into the sea; while two of the many species of Sequoia have come safely through all the geological changes and storms that have fallen upon them since Cretaceous times.

As Scotsman Muir elsewhere remarked,
Who wad ha thocht it?

Which is Which?
Three members of the bald cypress family of trees, the Taxodiaceae, are famous as 'redwoods.' These are the coast redwood of California and far southern Oregon, Sequoia sempervirens; the giant sequoia or big tree, Sequoiadendron giganteum, found at scattered locations in the Sierra Nevada of California only; and the dawn redwood, Metasequoia glyptostoboides, identified in the 1940s in central China. Of the three, the coast redwood is the tallest and by far the most widespread. The giant sequoia is the most massive and reaches the greatest ages. Fossils of the dawn redwood are found over much of the Northern Hemisphere.

Coastal Redwood   Giant Sequoia   Dawn Redwood

Burls at the base of red-wood trees are normal; big bulges of burl tissue higher on the trunks are, so to speak, mistakes. Wartlike, they seem neither to serve any purpose nor to do any harm. Muir Woods is known for its spectacular examples.

Redwood bark is thick—six to twelve inches on a mature tree—and is very fire resistant and insulating from heat. But ground fire can set the outer layers smoldering; vigorous flames can heat the bark enough in spots to kill the cambium, the living layer beneath. Later fires can then burn away bark and wood to create a scar, a cavity, or a hollow big enough to camp in—the pioneers called these 'goose-pens'.

S

Redwood Place: Of Fog and Fire

THERE IS FOG OVER REDWOOD CREEK this morning: moving in the tops, dampening hillside meadows, milling among the boles. A visitor asks: "Are you going to get any sun in here today?" Maybe. Maybe not. But if you find the fog dreary, you are not a redwood tree.

Redwoods require a humid, equable climate and cannot endure a pronounced summer drought. Only at the far northern end of the species' range, if there, is rainfall sufficient and distributed well enough around the year to give them what they need; at Muir Woods, annual rain averages only some 40 inches, nearly all of it falling between November and March. If there were no other source of moisture, by August the soil would be dry enough to start killing the redwoods.

But not long after the rains taper off, the summer fogs begin, pushing in and out almost daily, on some days barely admitting the pale outline of the sun. By keeping temperatures low, the fog slows evaporation from needles and ground. Droplets catch and condense on needles and leaves, sifting down in what is called 'fog-drip'—thought to contribute the equivalent of about ten extra inches of rain a year. It is even suspected (though not proven) that redwoods absorb fog's moisture directly into their needles, reversing the normal 'evapotranspiration' process by which plants lose water to air.

In the drier southern part of redwood country, Muir Woods included, winter rain and summer fog combined are not enough to guarantee a redwood climate. Here the trees are confined to spots made especially moist by the shape of the land—places that are both wind-sheltered and topographically shady.

Trees of Shade

Look at your shadow in sunlight. If you're standing anywhere north of the tropics, it will always be falling somewhat north of you—northwest in the morning, northeast in the evening, stubbily due north at noon. To put it another way, your north slope is shadier. So it is with hills. Their north-facing sides are shadier, therefore cooler, therefore more humid. And their northeast sides are even cooler than

Record-Size Trees
The tallest trees in the world are California coast redwoods. Just which individual trunk is the tallest is debatable and changeable, but several specimens in far northern California surpass 360 feet. The tallest at Muir Woods is a mere 253 feet; it stands in Bohemian Grove. The thickest local tree, a little over 13 feet through at chest height, is nearby. So rangers say, but caution that a really thorough inventory has never been done. To prevent trampling at their roots, the record trees are no longer singled out by signs.

their northwest ones, because whatever sun they get is morning sun, received before the air has gotten warm. In the high mountains, north and northeast exposures grow glaciers. In California coastal hills, you find redwood trees instead.

When you're walking in the shadows of Muir Woods, it seems that the redwood forest might go on forever. Leave the canyon floor, however, and you'll quickly see the workings of sun-angle or 'aspect.' If you take a trail to the right, you'll be climbing a south-facing hillside; the redwoods soon give way to a drier mixed evergreen forest, with such trees as oaks and orange-barked madrones. Take a trail to the shadier left hand, and the redwoods continue for half a mile, abruptly ceasing only when the windy crest is neared.

The redwood forest is one of five major vegetation communities that cover the watershed of Redwood Creek. The others are low, bristling chaparral; coastal scrub, a differing type of brushfield; mixed evergreen forest, including Douglas-fir, oaks, and madrone; and open hillside prairie. Each type gives way to others in a mosaic that can seem, at first, merely random. But each native plant and plant community grows where it can, where it must, where it fits. Like the redwood forest, each has its reasons.

Redwood Cones

This tallest of conifers has one of the smallest of cones, less than an inch wide and long. Compare the redwood cone on the right, above, to the giant sequoia cone on the left and the Douglas-fir cone in the middle. In the fall, each redwood cone releases 90 to 150 brown, flattened seeds. Fewer than 10 percent germinate, and only a very few seedlings survive the attack of fungus in the moist litter of an undisturbed forest floor. But where mineral soil is exposed—for instance, where a tree has fallen, or where a flood has either removed organic litter or buried it with silt—seedlings thrive. They also appear on downed logs where dust has settled to form pockets of soil.

People marvel at the age of the redwoods in Muir Woods. But specialists scratch their heads at the relative youthfulness of these trees.

The average lifespan of a big redwood, a redwood that makes it up into the full sunlight of the forest top or 'canopy,' is apparently about one thousand years. Not a few trees last twice that long. But in Muir Woods, there seem to be no trees older than the standard millennium. (It's rather like a human population with absolutely no one over seventy.) Why? There seem to be two possible answers.

First explanation: these redwoods are on the young side because, in this place, they die early. Redwood Canyon is less than outstanding redwood habitat. It may simply be a bit too dry here, a bit too windy, a bit too thin of soil, a bit too subject to droughts and periodic fires to allow the trees to reach a typical redwood life.

Second and more dramatic explanation: Muir Woods is young because it is new. The whole forest, this speculation goes, burned to the ground about a thousand years ago; it has been recovering ever since. It would follow that this is an adolescent redwood forest, with a more magnificent adulthood still ahead of it—barring another catastrophic fire.

The Ecology of Fire

Fire has certainly been here. Along the Muir Woods trails you'll find some trees fire blackened, some trees fire scarred, a few deeply fire hollowed, and several apparently fire killed—but with sprout circles rising around them. Before the 1800s, the Muir Woods canyon floor was probably singed several times a century. The last significant burn occurred around 1845.

Official attitudes toward fire in the forest have been changing. In the old days, it was simply the enemy, at all times to be prevented and extinguished. One early park superintendent of Muir Woods speculated happily that, due to fire protection, the trees might spread down Redwood Creek toward the coast (most unlikely). Then, as these matters began to be studied further in forests around the world, ecologists did a series of double takes.

They came to realize that, in many landscapes, fire is simply inevitable, and that, moreover, the attempt to prevent all fire sometimes only guarantees that more dead wood will be available for an eventual holocaust. They found further that certain species, certain landscapes, actually depend on fire for their maintenance. The giant sequoia of the Sierra Nevada, for example, would lose out to other trees if frequent, light fires did not sweep through the groves.

Do the coast redwoods, like their mountain relatives, depend on fire? It's a matter of debate. Plainly, this species does not need fire in order to reproduce: though seedlings root best on bare mineral soil, other forces than fire create the necessary openings in the

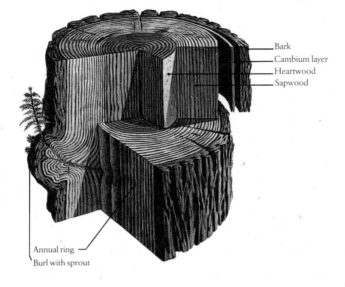

Bark
Cambium layer
Heartwood
Sapwood

Annual ring
Burl with sprout

Not all redwood bark looks alike. In the unusual 'curly' redwood, above center, a wavy grain runs through both bark and wood.

forest, and there is always sprout reproduction to fall back on. But there is some evidence that occasional fires are healthy for this forest, particularly in controlling the heart-root rot *Poria sequoiae*. And there is the usual concern that the exclusion of small fires will store up fuel for a big one. Fire ecology is a complex subject. It is dangerous to proclaim broad rules; every community, sometimes every site, seems to respond in its own ways. The Park Service is anxious to learn more.

It is conceivable that, someday, fire will deliberately be reintroduced to the core of Muir Woods. But nobody wants it to happen by accident. Other parts of Mount Tamalpais, where the vegetation is more fire-prone, burn with some regularity. Several big blazes, spreading down the mountain, have been turned back just short of the National Monument boundary. Now the Park Service is working to surround the core of Muir Woods with a fuelbreak, a zone where there is little woody ground debris to carry flames along from tree to tree. They will build that fuelbreak with the help of the very force it is meant to contain. Small, controlled fires, set in cool weather, seem to behave as intended, smoldering rather than blazing, and consuming only the twigs and duff.

CONTROLLED FIRES ALSO SERVE as experiments. Carefully watching what happens during and after these burns, researchers should be able to draw some conclusions about the ways in which this particular redwood forest responds to fire, and what its future management should be.

In a mature redwood forest, only two or three new stems per acre per century make it up into the full sunlight of the forest top or 'canopy.' But for this long-lived species, that's all it takes to keep the forest thriving.

Spotted owl country. The owl is one of a number of bird and animal species that live in and depend on complex, usually ancient forests.

Northern Spotted Owls

Strix occidentalis caurina *is a medium-sized owl, brown of eye and brown of feather, its plumage flecked with white. It is famous as an 'indicator species,' representative of all the wild things that live in and depend on complex forests. Muir Woods National Monument has all the things the owls need: lofty trees and lesser ones of several species; broken tops, snags, and cavities for nesting; open air for flight between the lowest branches and the forest floor; and logs and debris on the ground to house the owls' staple food, the dusky-footed wood rat.*

The Redwood Creek watershed apparently has a single breeding pair of spotted owls and has had a single pair at least since 1934, when people first started noticing. The 1,000-acre territory of that pair includes all the National Monument and considerable land outside. Home base seems to be near the confluence of Redwood Creek and Fern Creek.

When the young of the year mature, these fledglings must find territories elsewhere. They probably succeed, for Marin County, with its extensive parks, streams, reservoirs, and conifer forests, has a lot of good owl country. Owl specialists believe there are some twenty or thirty pairs in this area.

The owl hunts at night and isn't easily observed. Its characteristic call, resembling a very gentle bark, is quite unlike the classic owl hoot.

∫

Redwood Creek

THERE ARE, ACCORDING TO THE U.S. Geological Survey, 22 streams in California named Redwood Creek. The Redwood Creek that drains the bony flank of Mount Tamalpais and passes through Muir Woods on its course to the sea, three miles below the sequoias, is among the smallest. Larger streams in redwood country make corridors through their forests, opening sky; this stream flows within its forest, its waters cooled by redwood shade and carrying brown redwood needles, yellow redwood pollen, green sprigs blown from the redwood tops above.

It's diverting to walk the park with an eye to the water. I begin at the lower of the two Muir Woods parking lots, among the broad-leafed buckeye trees, and head upstream. At first the creek is inaccessible, moving swiftly between banks that are deeply cut though hung with fern. But just as you start seeing redwoods on the opposite bank, the scene changes. The streambanks grow shallower; the water comes closer with its shift and gleam.

Start noticing the creek and it seems to get bigger, to fully inhabit its narrow slot of a canyon. It dug this valley, after all; it laid down this soil. Curving back and forth from hillside to ferny hillside, it defines where the redwoods are: the biggest trees grow on the fertile alluvial points inside those curves. Bohemian Grove, one of the two named redwood groups in the park, fills a flat on the left bank, as you walk upstream; Cathedral Grove is on a right-hand flat.

Gentle stream-corridor in rugged hills...it is so typical a site for large redwoods in this southern part of their range that you wonder: Have the trees merely occupied these places, or do they in some manner help to create them? The latter is possible. Fallen branches and boles, slow to decay, certainly act as checkdams on these streams, causing them to pause in pools and drop gravels, silts and sands, causing them, too, to overflow their banks in winter floods and level and enrich the surrounding soil.

Natural dams and seasonal flooding, then, are basic to Muir Woods. But it took the National Park Service a few decades to catch on.

Every few years, it seems, a big storm drenches the watershed of Redwood Creek, sending down a flood that goes beyond exciting and commences to alarm. Banks erode. Streamside alders topple. Now and then a redwood falls. Today's park rangers regard such events as part of the territory, but their predecessors did not. After such a flood in 1924, a campaign was begun to keep the creek in bounds, first of all by keeping it free of fallen branches and debris. "I got everything out but three large stumps before my funds gave out," an early manager wrote proudly. But the taming of Redwood Creek really got going in 1933, when the New Deal public works programs brought an army of government labor. Between 1933 and 1938, the Civilian Conservation Corps (CCC) lined almost the entire length of the creek within Muir Woods with rockwork 'revetments,' handsome mortarless rock banks, still obvious in many places. CCC workers also installed log checkdams to replace untidy natural ones, and here and there they dumped a load of boulders to create a scenic artificial rapid. Any debris that got into the stream on its own, of course, was zealously removed.

Thirty years later, government researchers in the Pacific Northwest and elsewhere began to take a serious look at wild creeks and the processes at work within them. They zeroed in especially on the role of fallen logs and branches in such streams and found, to put it simply, that untidy streams work better (and contain more fish).

Word spread. About 1980, it reached Muir Woods. Since then the tendency has been to leave Redwood Creek to itself, so far as safety permits. Trees and boughs that fall into the creek now stay there. When the old rockwork sheds stones into the stream, there the stones lie. When the creek swirls out of its banks, leaving drifts of silt among the ferns, the park staff applauds. And if some few visitors wonder why things aren't kept rather neater (sometimes expressing sympathy: 'I guess they cut your budget, huh?'), they see the point immediately when informed.

Salamanders

The moist green places under redwood trees are perfect habitat for fragile-skinned amphibians, including the California newt, the California slender salamander, the Ensatina salamander, and the Pacific giant salamander, below (it is redwood colored and has a tiny doglike bark). These creatures are seen most often in the wet season, in or near quiet streams, in damp cavities, or under rotting logs or litter.

Salmon and Trout

Steelhead trout and silver salmon in little Redwood Creek? You may not see them, but whenever you look, they're there: transparent newly hatched "fry" in schools, quick solitary "fingerlings," groups of adults returned from the ocean to spawn. Both these species are anadromous: they live much of their lives at sea but return to fresh water to reproduce.

Silver or coho salmon, *Oncorhynchus kisutch*, hatch in the spring from tiny orange eggs concealed in the bottom gravel. They feed on small aquatic animals, insect larvae fallen into the stream, and each other. They survive the summer drought in lingering pools and threads of water. When the rains come back they begin making their way down to the sea, reaching it in April or May of their second year.

About one in 50 lives to swim in salt water. The fish are now about three inches long.

The salmon spend the next two to four years at sea, spreading out over much of the western Pacific and mingling with an Asian population of their species. But at the end of that time, they return not only to the correct continent but almost always to the very creek in which they were spawned. When the fall rains break the sand-bar at Muir Beach, the survivors—forty to one hundred fish—re-enter the stream and labor their way up the current to the headwaters, in and near Muir Woods.

If you watch the creek at the right time of year—from late December to the middle of March—and if you are lucky, you may see the precise, intense, repeated rituals of spawning. Or you may see dilapidated, 'spawned out' fish lingering in eddies, stranded on the bank, or floating off downstream. Like all Pacific salmon, the silver dies after it spawns.

Steelhead are the ocean-going race of rainbow trout, *Oncorhynchus mykiss*. They spawn a little later than salmon, hatch a little later, and spend two years, not one, in fresh water. They also do not die after one spawning but make several round trips to the ocean.

Is Redwood Creek a good stream for salmon and trout? If you compare it with other modern streams, the answer is: Yes, this habitat is excellent. If you compare it with what it once was and what it could be, the answer is: Not yet.

Over the years, the lagoon at its mouth, a brackish estuary where fish could feed and adjust as they switched from fresh to salt water, has almost vanished. Water has been drawn off for local agriculture, cutting summer flows. And in Muir Woods itself, long years of conscientious streambed cleaning have impoverished the habitat.

BUT LATELY THE NATIONAL PARK Service has been working to restore Redwood Creek, not only in Muir Woods but at its mouth as well (also federal parkland). Because no regular fish census is taken, success can't be proven by the numbers. Still, park employees, watching year after year, feel no doubt that they're seeing more and more of these, the water travellers.

Horsetails thrive along Redwood Creek.

Female salmon, silvery all over with black spots on the back, are hard to distinguish from steelhead trout of either sex. But after some time in fresh water, male silver salmon develop elongated snouts and flanks the color of a fresh-cut redwood log. In Redwood Creek, where the spawning grounds are a quick trip from the sea, few of the fish fully develop these characteristics. The first runs of the season typically contain only salmon; from February on, steelhead predominate. Look for either in clear water a few days after a rain.

Despite some earlier flood control engineering, Redwood Creek in Muir Woods is one of the least-altered streams in the San Francisco Bay Area.

The smaller redwoods of the hillside forest.

§

William Kent's Woods

MUIR WOODS AS WE HAVE IT today is in a sense an artificial, accidental treasure.

This forest, for all its massive loveliness, is a rather average specimen of old-growth redwoods. You won't find here the tallest redwoods, nor the thickest, nor the oldest, nor the lushest woodland floor. Any of a hundred local canyons might equally well have been the site of a federal redwood park. But, by the late 1800s, those other canyons had all been logged. Human beings, by cutting down all but one of the prominent ancient redwood stands within reach of San Francisco Bay, conferred uniqueness on the one they spared.

At that, it was a pretty near thing.

Muir Woods survived the logging boom of the middle 1800s by topographical luck. The steep little ridge that lies between it and the town of Mill Valley was far more an obstacle then; the seacove at the mouth of Redwood Creek was a poor ship landing. As early as 1870 the grove was drawing notice as a rarity, but it stayed in private hands.

One chance to preserve it was missed in the 1890s, when the Bohemian Club came, saw, and shivered. A member of that wealthy fraternity had actually purchased land at the woods on speculation, hoping to resell it to the Club for a permanent encampment. That September, the Club gathered at the spot still called Bohemian Grove to celebrate their elaborate annual 'Midsummer Jinks.' (Their central prop was a lathe-and-plaster Buddha seventy feet high.) But the following night under fog-wet canvas was cold enough, Club records state, to "freeze the male evidence off a brass monkey." At a meeting later that fall, the members refused to accept the site, and the would-be benefactor found another buyer.

Ten years later, logging appeared imminent.

Enter the hero of the story, the man for whom Muir Woods is notably not named, William Kent. A man of ambition, conscience and wealth, Kent had large plans for the Mount Tamalpais region. As the owner of extensive lands there, he hoped to profit from the tourist trade. As a conservationist, he wanted to see founded on

Miwoks

Miwoks made shell beads out of clam shells. The tribe had a village at the mouth of Redwood Creek, now known as Muir Beach. There is little evidence of their presence in Muir Woods, but they would certainly have come here for salmon and other natural products.

the mountain a national park "on the lines of Yellowstone." Redwood Canyon was included in the plan.

In 1903, at a meeting in Mill Valley, Kent called into being a Mount Tamalpais National Park Association. Among those present was Gifford Pinchot, the great forester. Almost instantly there came a query from the current owner, the Tamalpais Land and Water Company: Would Kent himself buy these redwoods to save them from the saw?

Kent, whose fortune consisted largely of unprofitable landholdings, did not jump at the offer: "I informed him that I could not afford to own any more white elephants, and wanted to know why the...Company did not preserve [the trees] themselves."

You won't see the rare pileated woodpecker, but it's nice to know it's there.

But Kent did visit the woods. "The beauty of the place attracted me, and got on my mind, and I could not forget the situation." Finally, in 1905, he plunged. He bought not only the core of Muir Woods but the entire holdings of the Land and Water Company, 611 acres in all, for the discounted but still-formidable sum of $45,000. His wife, Elizabeth Thatcher Kent, recalls the answer she got when she questioned the expense: "If we lost all the money we have and saved these trees, it would be worthwhile, wouldn't it?" Kent may just have meant it. Later, only half-joking, he would use similar words to urge a California governor to buy additional redwood parks at any cost: "Damn the public schools, Bill! Shut them up for a year and save those trees!"

One year after Kent acquired his forest, San Francisco lay in ashes in the aftermath of earthquake and fire, waiting to be built all over again with redwood lumber. But none of that lumber, now, would come from Redwood Canyon.

Kent hoped to get his money back by making the grove a rustic private resort. He struck a deal with the operators of the famous tourist railroad that then climbed from Mill Valley to the summit of Mount Tamalpais. If they would build a branch line down to the woods, he would construct a hotel and lease the whole canyon to the railroad for annual rent and a share of the ticket sales.

But other interests had their eye on the canyon. Late in 1907, a water company in the nearby town of Sausalito announced plans to dam Redwood Creek near the present Monument entrance, drowning the main redwood groves, or rather their stumps, for of course they would first be logged. The company went to court to condemn the land. Kent hunted for a way out. A friend in the federal government called his attention to a new law, the Antiquities Act of 1906, which allowed the president to set up parklike National Monuments without going through Congress. Was this the saving tool?

Gift to the Nation

Putting together a portfolio of photographs and articles about Redwood Canyon, Kent approached two of Theodore Roosevelt's cabinet members. Interior Secretary James Garfield was not much help. It was the secretary of agriculture, none other than Kent's acquaintance Gifford Pinchot, who took the case to the president.

Late in 1907, William Kent gave 295 acres of his Redwood Canyon property to the nation; on January 9, 1908, Roosevelt declared the land a National Monument, inviolable. In a public exchange of letters, the president urged that the monument be named Kent Woods, for the donor; but Kent insisted that it bear instead the name of conservationist John Muir. Muir accepted in solemn Victorian phrases, describing the gift as a "credit and encouragement to God."

His great donation to the people did not end Kent's connection with Muir Woods. He still owned much land around the central groves, including the Monument's parking lot and the springs that gave it drinking water. For a number of years after the donation, Kent paid a caretaker to run the property. Even when the government finally took up that burden, the caretaker was 'Kent's man.'

Kent was also the reluctant owner of the rugged stage road that brought those people to the park who did not come on foot or by train. He had offered the road as part of the gift, but the government preferred to let him keep on bearing the expense of maintenance. Finally Kent began collecting tolls.

Birds of Muir Woods

Redwood forests aren't famous for birds, but Muir Woods has more than a few. Everybody notices the bright and noisy Steller's jay, here in summer and a great scavenger, and the ravens when they caw above the trees. Most people spot Oregon juncos and the small melodious winter wren, busy along the water. Brown creepers, nuthatches, and bushtits work up and down the trunks. In summer, a pair of mallards regularly shows up in the creek, and occasionally great blue herons come up to fish. In the fall, warblers and flycatchers, golden-crowned kinglets and varied thrushes arrive in flocks.

Near the monument entrance, outside the redwood groves, you'll see scrub jays instead of Steller's, and hear great horned owls at evening instead of spotted owls. You may see Cooper's hawks on the hunt, and in early summer, quail rustling by with their comical squadrons of young.

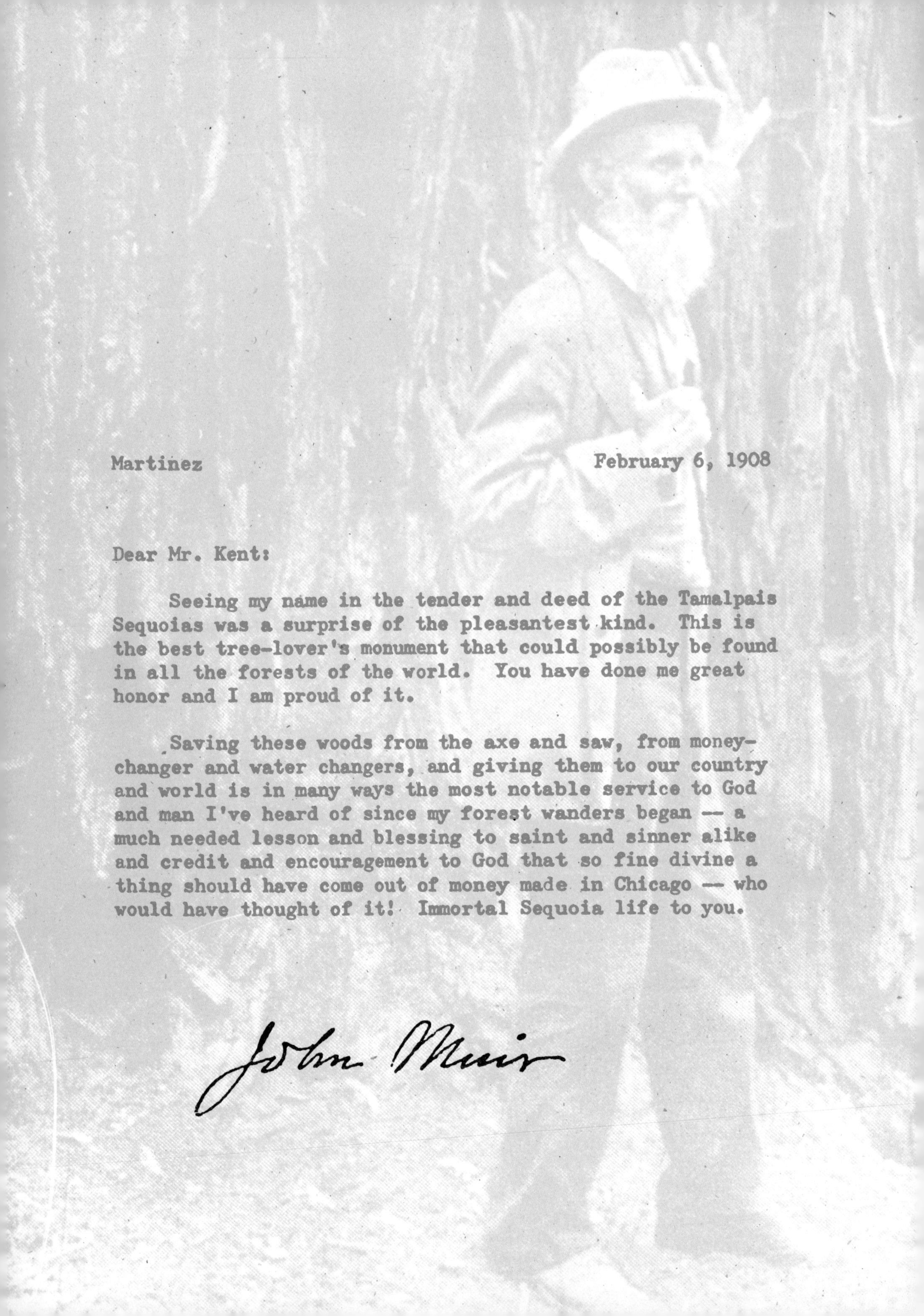

Martinez   February 6, 1908

Dear Mr. Kent:

    Seeing my name in the tender and deed of the Tamalpais
Sequoias was a surprise of the pleasantest kind. This is
the best tree-lover's monument that could possibly be found
in all the forests of the world. You have done me great
honor and I am proud of it.

    Saving these woods from the axe and saw, from money-
changer and water changers, and giving them to our country
and world is in many ways the most notable service to God
and man I've heard of since my forest wanders began — a
much needed lesson and blessing to saint and sinner alike
and credit and encouragement to God that so fine divine a
thing should have come out of money made in Chicago — who
would have thought of it! Immortal Sequoia life to you.

                    John Muir

Naming Redwoods
It used to be standard practice to name redwood trees for people, causes, and events. There are trees at Muir Woods named for William Kent, Gifford Pinchot, and Ralph Waldo Emerson; a plaque for FDR and the United Nations; even a tree for 'pioneer optometrist Andrew J. Cross.' Such labelling has gradually fallen out of favor, but a Bicentennial tree—precisely as old as the nation—was identified in 1976.

The vistas, verticals and silences of a redwood forest summon an image as irresistible as it is trite: there is always a Cathedral Grove. Bohemian Grove is named for San Francisco's Bohemian Club, whose members spent an uncomfortable night here in 1892.

From 1911 to 1918, Kent served in Congress. Back home in the 1920s, he plugged away on his project of blanketing Mount Tamalpais with parks. He offered large tracts to the National Monument (only a few acres were accepted) and, just before his death in 1928, to the new Mount Tamalpais State Park. The park-building process he started rolled on decade after decade until, today, the entire rugged region is in public ownership as part of a still more vast greenbelt extending from the Golden Gate north to Point Reyes. Parts of that greenbelt are state parks, parts are protected watershed land owned by a local district, and parts belong to the Golden Gate National Recreation Area (GGNRA), established in 1972. Muir Woods National Monument itself, despite its earlier and separate origin, is now part of the GGNRA.

William Kent's name is found at only one spot in Muir Woods: up the canyon of Fern Creek, on a plaque on a rock beside a gigantic Douglas-fir. Volunteers from the Tamalpais Conservation Club placed this memorial in 1929. This tree, Kent's favorite, was actually higher than any of the Monument's redwoods—until the winter of 1981-82, when a storm tore off the top of the tree.

Namesake John Muir

One Muir Woods visitor very sensibly asked: "What's a Muir?"

John Muir. 1838-1914. Scientist, farmer, inventor, adventurer, canny businessman: but above all, American conservationist. Born in Scotland; raised in Wisconsin. Reborn, he said, in 1867, when a factory accident left him temporarily blind.

Lying in darkness, Muir made a promise to himself: if his sight came back, he would work at a trade no more but would spend the rest of his life exploring the bright world. "I might have become a millionaire," he wrote. "I chose to become a tramp." His wanderings would indeed be prodigious, but one place above all was to become his spiritual home: the Yosemite country in California's Sierra Nevada Range.

Wherever Muir went, he saw the American landscape being abused, especially by brutal overgrazing, uncontrolled logging, and rapacious mining practices. His anger grew, and he began to write.

After an interlude in which he started a family and grumblingly but profitably raised fruit, Muir made conservation his full-time career. His increasingly eloquent nature articles and polemics appeared in every influential journal. He argued and lobbied and pleaded and pressured and fought. And people listened. Largely due to his work, Yosemite became a national park in 1890.

In 1892, Muir became the first president of the Sierra Club. With the Club he saw millions of acres of public land become national parks and national forests. And he kept on writing. By the

Wildflowers
In the low light of the red-wood forest, flowers are not abundant or showy, but there are plenty of things that bloom. In March and April, nobody misses the low Pacific trillium, with its three white petals darkening slowly to rose. Azalea bushes along the creek bloom in summer, their masses of creamy flowers smelling as lovely as they look. At your feet, the ubiquitous cloverlike Oregon oxalis, above, bears pale pink flowers eight months of the year.

California Laurel

You still occasionally see in print the old fable about the 'Oregon myrtle' tree: that it grows nowhere on earth but in Oregon and in Palestine. In fact, the myrtle or California laurel, Umbellularia californica, grows widely along the west coast of North America and not at all in the Old World. Two things are striking about it: its sharply aromatic leaf and the way it sprawls and falls when it grows in shady places. Laurel trunks and branches lean toward any available sunlight, stretching out and out until their weight topples the tree. But fallen laurel boles usually keep growing, striking new roots where needed and sending up rows of new stems.

time Muir Woods was named for him in 1908, John Muir had helped to create a whole new climate of opinion.

Leaders at Odds

Muir's worst defeat came at the place he cared about most of all. In 1913, Congress voted to let the City of San Francisco invade Yosemite National Park and build a dam on the Tuolumne River, drowning Hetch Hetchy, "the other Yosemite Valley." Among the voices for that dam was Gifford Pinchot; among the votes for it was Congressman William Kent, the savior of Redwood Creek six years before.

The bitter Hetch Hetchy debate convinced all sides that there needed to be a law defining the uses of parks and creating, for the first time, a special office to manage places like Muir Woods and Yosemite: the National Park Service. The man who introduced the Park Service act of 1916: William Kent.

Puzzling? Ironic? Neither, really. However simple the conservation issues of the early 1900s look in hindsight—however clearly we may think we see who was right, wrong, or inconsistent—they were not simple then. It was a time when foundations were being laid. The people who laid them often disagreed.

There is at Muir Woods a great tree dedicated to Gifford Pinchot, without whose help, indeed, it might no longer stand. The Sierra Club placed a plaque at its base in 1910. William Kent served lunch. Pinchot was not present. He was furious that Muir Woods had not been given to his Forest Service for management. Muir was not present. He despised Pinchot as a man who saw forests only as sources of lumber and other commercial values.

Kent, Muir, Pinchot: Muir Woods needed them all.

Hunting the Balance:
The National Park Service at Muir Woods

THE 1916 LAW ESTABLISHING the National Park Service told the new agency to do two things in its domains: first, "to conserve the scenery and the natural and historic objects and the wildlife therein;" and, second, "to provide for the enjoyment of the same."

It had occurred to no one yet that conservation and enjoyment might sometimes pull against each other—that it takes hard and intelligent work to conserve what large numbers of people come to enjoy. The tiny and hugely popular park called Muir Woods National Monument would quickly prove the point.

Early in its career as a park, Redwood Canyon was an open place, welcoming, sometimes crowded, with every comfort available under the big red trees and no one to tell you not to trample the moss. At one time you could take your car clear through it. There were as many as sixteen footbridges across the creek (compare the current four). Picnic tables and restrooms stood everywhere among the trees. Groups of several hundred sang songs around great fires.

There was a price.

As early as the 1920s, it became apparent that the web and texture of the forest floor were fraying. Where ferns had been, and all the wide-leafed, subtly flowering things, now were trampled paths and swatches of bare dirt. Erosion was uncovering redwood roots. The distressed trees were sprouting, but nobody noticed, for the traffic stripped the new shoots off as fast as they appeared. There was also wholesale 'poaching' of such valued plants as ferns and trilliums. The five finger ferns that had lined the creekbank disappeared entirely.

Park Service files tell a repeated story of alarm, attempted corrective action, cautious optimism, and alarm renewed. In 1923, at William Kent's behest, the road through the grove was closed to cars. Overnight camping was curtailed in 1924. The 1929 demise of the Muir Woods and Mount Tamalpais Railway took some of the foot traffic out of the upper groves—and shifted it to the lower ones. In 1933, fires were banned. Barton J. Herschler, Monument Custodian during that decade, forbade ballgames in the groves and was "most vigilant in

No Holes Bored
"Where's the drive-through tree?" It's a common question at the gate. There's nothing like that here (the nearest one is several hundred miles north). There used to be a naturally formed walk-through tree, now fallen.

apprehending 'fern-pickers and initial-carvers." In the late '30s, though, when the Golden Gate Bridge opened and the tollgates were taken off the Muir Woods road, use abruptly tripled, and so did the wear and tear.

In 1942, in the middle of a heavy rainstorm, a young ranger named Lawson Brainerd sloshed into the park and started clearing culverts. He would work there for 23 years under six different superintendents, gaining deep knowledge of these woods and also building that special kind of influence that belongs to the permanent second-echelon employee. From the start, Brainerd pressed himself and his superiors to new diligence in countering what he called "human erosion."

His first target was the picnic tables that still stood in many spots among the trees. ("Food in the mouth and a few ants," Brainerd said, "and you can have a picnic anywhere.") In 1953, a quarter century after removal was first suggested, the park took out the last of these. In the same decade, most of the numerous Redwood Creek bridges came down, and the park pulled out the signs that had made special attractions of the tallest tree and others that were notable or curious. Each tree had been the center of a trampled zone and, indeed, the object of a certain amount of vandalism.

Brainerd made it a project to rebuild groundcover. Visiting side canyons, he carried down cuttings and seedlings. He brought down sword fern, the characteristic low plant of the woods, with its stiff

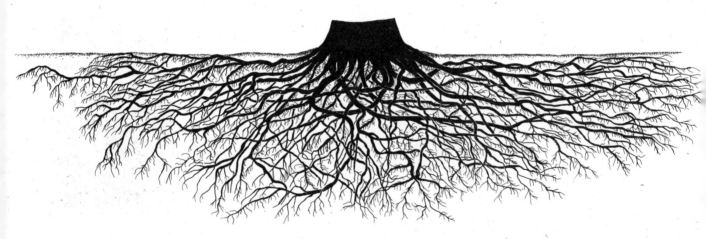

Compared to the great mass of its trunk, the roots of a typical redwood tree are puny. They don't go deep for water but spread out shallowly just below the surface, gathering moisture from fog-drip as well as from rain. If a flood deposits silt and actually raises the ground level, the trunk can send out a fresh layer of roots just below the new surface. Shallow roots don't make for stability. In a forest, mutual wind-shelter and interlocking roots keep the trees firm; but if part of the stand is cut away, trees at the new edge will topple by the dozen.

Poison oak, above, is a plant to avoid at Muir Woods. Just brushing by a Toxicodendron diversilobum *bush, you can pick up some of its toxic oil and suffer, hours or days later, a miserable rash. There's not much poison oak under the big redwoods, but watch for it along remoter hillside trails: a shrub or vine with oaklike leaves in threes, leafless in winter. If exposed to it, wash thoroughly.*

To the right, a Muir Woods sampler: new redwood foliage; oyster fungus; redwood saplings rooted on a fallen trunk.

green angular fronds. He transplanted *Woodwardia fimbriata*, the intricate giant chain fern. Planted five finger fern on denuded creekbanks. Set out wild ginger and coaxed oxalis over barren ground. This process has continued ever since.

There were other plants that had to be discouraged. Muir Woods is close to urban neighborhoods and former ranches, and from these spread species that had never been part of the natural fabric of the woods. Down from the site of the Muir Woods Inn came the tough and pretty forget-me-not, named for its hooked, cuff-clinging seed. On the valley floor, it threatened to replace the native oxalis. From the ridge to the east came the virulent Scotch broom, thickets of which now cover miles of Marin County. Out of Australia came the bluegum eucalyptus, a handsome tree but one not wanted in a park devoted to native flora. Himalaya blackberry, poison hemlock, star thistle, pampas grass: the list of undesirables goes on and on. So does the process of pulling out the invaders. The central groves, at least, are now nearly free of them.

The Return of the Woods

But despite all these efforts, Muir Woods did not entirely lose its sad and trampled look. Increased visitation (up to 784,000 by 1967) largely swamped the restoration work. Meanwhile, national attitudes were changing. People were taking a fresh look at the National Park idea. Critics pointed out that the 1916 act did not, in truth, put recreation on an equal footing with protection of nature: parks are to be made available for public enjoyment "in such a manner and by such means as will leave them unimpaired for the enjoyment of future generations." Despite decades of diligence, Muir Woods was failing this test.

Plainly, if the park was to welcome its always-increasing public, the style of the welcome would have to undergo a further change. What had begun as a playground would have to complete its evolution into something more jealously cherished: indeed, a species of museum.

In 1968, Muir Woods began a process of narrowing and defining its trails. Where people had wandered among the trees, now there were a few specific paths, lined with substantial split-rail fences and—to protect the shallow-lying redwood roots—surfaced with asphalt. It was paradoxical but unavoidable: to better protect this piece of the forest primeval, parts of it had to be paved.

It worked.

Walk out to Cathedral Grove, where the trail splits around an island of trees. Until 1971, that cluster stood in a desert of trampled ground. Then the fences went up. By the following May, new redwood shoots were appearing: "probably the first permitted to develop to this visible stage in seventy years," the Superintendent reported in 1972. Rangers planted redwood seedlings on the island, too, and dozens of

Mammals of Muir Woods
The brown bears and California grizzlies are long gone from Muir Woods. The mammals you're most likely to see are sharp-faced raccoons and hesitant, high-stepping black-tailed deer (perhaps munching on oxalis). The largest predators are bobcats and gray foxes, above. Most numerous are the rodents: gray squirrels, Sonoma chipmunks, valley pocket gophers, deer mice, shrews, and others.

The Rails and the Inns

MT TAMALPAIS
GRAVITY
6

Today the front door of Muir Woods is the southern, downstream end. But from 1908 to 1929, the park faced the other way. Most visitors came from the north, and most came either on foot or on the Mount Tamalpais and Muir Woods Railway.

In service since 1892, this famous railway line steamed all the way up the local mountain, mounting 2,300 feet on a route whose magnificent kinkiness made it 'The Crookedest Railroad In the World.' In 1907, the line sprouted a branch toward the new Muir Woods National Monument. Its first terminus was a flat well north of the Monument boundary, now known as Camp Alice Eastwood, where stood the Muir or Muir Woods Inn; a carriage road, used as a broad trail today, linked down to the redwoods.

Some of the trains that ran down to the Inn were unpowered 'gravity cars.' Passengers loved these trips, the almost silent, effortless passages down chaparral-sleek slopes toward the shaggy canyon floor. The trips back up, of course, required laboring engines.

People who didn't come by rail, if old statistics can be believed, came largely on foot; but auto travel soon was important, too. The first car, a Winton, rattled down from the ridge in the winter of 1907–08 on a rougher version of today's main access road. Once in the Monument, carriages and cars could drive right through the redwoods and, if they liked, on up to the Muir Inn.

In 1913 an internal fire destroyed the main Inn building; most of its outlying cabins followed a few weeks later when a major brushfire swept over

Tamalpais. One carload of rail passengers made it down that mountain, a contemporary story went, huddling under cloths soaked in champagne. (A witness insists, though, that the wine was drunk.) But at the Inn site, the remaining liquor supply was poured on the ground to keep it from distracting the fire crews.

After the fire, the railroad line was pushed nearer the valley floor and a second Muir Inn constructed. Paths and stairs led down to the redwoods. To see the second Inn site, you can walk a few hundred yards up the old carriage road, following signs to Camp Eastwood; the Inn stood at a gentle bend just beyond the second sharp switchback. The railroad grade, heavily overgrown, parallels the carriage road on a higher alignment, crossing it near the notch called the Plevin Cut.

In 1929, another great fire burned on Tamalpais. One fire-fighting crew, nearly trapped by the flames, escaped to Muir Woods Inn on the gravity car. But the Muir Woods branch never saw another train, and the whole Railway soon shut down for good, due less to fire damage than to the good summit highway that had begun to compete with it.

Abandoned, the Inn was torn down in 1932. Lumber and fittings wound up in several unremarkable park buildings. The name, too, was salvaged. The third 'Muir Woods Inn' was a restaurant and tavern across the road from the Monument entrance (the building still stands). In 1969, this operation moved into the park. Buy a sandwich: the tray it sits on bears the logo of the Muir Woods Inn.

The Inn in 1908.

ferns. This time, protected behind fences, the new plants took hold. To a casual eye, this spot, like a dozen other former wastelands in Muir Woods, looks aboriginal.

It took a few more years to take the next step: to break the long-established habit of housekeeping—keeping the forest floor tidy, free of straggling branches and brushy deadfalls. Yet it was no secret that debris builds soil, feeds insects, draws birds. Salamanders, shrews, the wood rats that feed the owls, all need low-lying 'clutter.' Finally, about 1980, the automatic cleanup ceased. Now, unless there's a specific reason for removing them, things that fall in the forest are left to lie.

The new untidiness may spoil a few photographic compositions. But to a naturalist's eye, Muir Woods today is looking better and working better than it has for the larger part of a century. The old bare stingy look is fading. There seem to be more flowers, more insects, and (though birds aren't prominent in any redwood forest) more sparrows, juncos, towhees, wrens. Some characteristic plants that had all but disappeared—minty yerba buena, for example, and wild ginger with its curious brown three-tendril flower—now seem to be everywhere.

Muir Woods still has to be called a recovering forest. But year by year it seems to be fuller of that green and lively light, shady yet somehow never dim, that the dusty eye takes in as a thirsty throat takes in water.

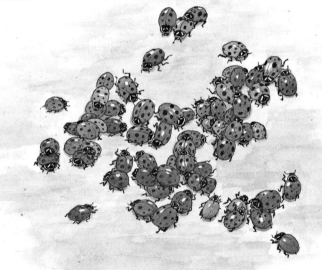

Ladybugs

A notable insect at Muir Woods is the 'convergent ladybug.' These orange-and-black beetles hatch in inland valleys in the spring, stuff themselves with aphids and pollen (one meal per lifetime), and migrate on the wind to cooler sites. In October at Muir Woods they clump together in great masses, especially along the Bootjack and Fern Creek trails. In late winter they mate and return to the inland valleys to lay eggs and die.

Each winter, the sleek Pacific madrone, Arbutus menziesii, *sheds its bright orange outer bark in papery curls, exposing a smooth green skin that dries to orange again. At Muir Woods, madrones grow in the mixed evergreen woods bordering the pure redwood stands.*

A Zoo for Trees?

What would John Muir think today if he saw the woods that bear his name? Certainly, he wouldn't confuse the place with the true wild places that he loved. Fenced, paved, interpreted, this park is in some ways very artificial. It has even been dismissed as a 'zoo for trees.'

Yet the zoo comparison is almost an inversion of the truth. In a zoo, people circulate among animals that are confined and far from their native places. Here, the forest is where it always was. It is the human visitors who, for the sake of the trees, agree to confine themselves.

And if this is not a wild park, no place to grasp 'the freedom of the hills,' it has another function. It is a contact point, a place of meeting. For many millions of visitors, it is the first redwood grove they have seen. For many more, it is the first encounter with the national park idea: that there are places where the preservation of an ecosystem—down to the last tree, shrub, shrew, newt, fish, and owl—is paramount. Both the trees and the idea, in truth, take a little getting used to.

William Kent, we remember, once urged the governor to close schools and save forests. He didn't go on to observe that forests can also be schools. John Muir would have made much of that point, had he been along.

If Muir visited his woods today? He probably wouldn't care much for the parking lot. Once past that and homing into the green, watching the people watch the trees, hearing in unknown languages the upward lilt of awe, I suspect he would declare himself well pleased.

Overheard on the trail:
"It's not so quiet here. I guess it's the wind."

"And us."

About Muir Woods National Monument

Muir Woods National Monument is open every day of the year from 8 a.m. until sunset. For more information, call (415) 388-2595.

What to see:
The visitor center at the entrance has exhibits and an excellent selection of brochures, books, and other information on Muir Woods.

Trails range from easy, short loops to more vigorous day hikes. Easy, paved main trails loop through the redwoods on the forest floor and are wheelchair and stroller accessible. Longer hikes range from 2 to 9 miles and offer varying levels of difficulty. Be sure to pick up a map at the visitor center.

Trails include the Redwood Groves Loop (2 miles/easy); the Fern Creek Loop (4 miles/moderate); the Ben Johnson Loop (4.5 miles/moderate); the Dipsea Loop (8.5 miles/strenuous); the Hassle-Free Loop (4.5 miles/ moderate); and the Frank Valley Trail (one way: 2.5 miles/easy).

When to visit:
The best time to visit is weekdays, or early or late on weekend days. Summer weekends are very crowded. You can avoid parking problems by hiking in from other park areas.

What to wear:
Dress warmly, it's always cool among the redwoods, and wear comfortable walking shoes.

Suggested Reading

A Guide to the Trails of Muir Woods. Golden Gate National Park Association, 1991.

Becking, Rudolf W., A Pocket Flora of the Redwood Forest. Island Press, 1982.

Fairley, Lincoln. Mount Tamalpais: A History. Scottwall Associates, 1987.

Kelly, David. Secrets of the Old Growth Forest. Gibbs Smith Publisher, 1990 (revised edition).

Lyons, Kathleen and Mary Beth Cuneo-Lazaneo. Plants of the Coast Redwood Region. Looking Press, 1988.

Western hounds's tongue

About the Author
Among environmental writer John Hart's many books are *San Francisco's Wilderness Next Door*, a history of the Golden Gate National Recreation Area and environs; *Walking Softly in the Wilderness: The Sierra Club Guide to Backpacking*; and *The Climbers*, a poetry collection.

The Golden Gate National Park Association wishes to thank the staff of the Golden Gate National Recreation Area who helped review and produce this publication.

GGNPA Production Management
Charles Money
Greg Moore

Editor
Nora L. Deans

Design
Nancy E. Koc

Photography
All photography by Brenda Tharp except:

GGNPA Archives (pages 30, 40, 41)
Catherine Karnow (page 27)
Larry Ulrich (page 14)

Illustrations
Karen Montgomery (page 4)
National Park Service (page 16)
Lawrence Ormsby (pages 7, 20-bottom, 23, 29, 36, 38, 39-top, 46)
Claus Sievert (pages 1, 3, 10, 13, 14, 19, 20-top, 21, 28, 34, 35, 39-bottom, 42)

Set in Sabon Antiqua on an Apple Macintosh with Quark Express 3.0

Printed in Hong Kong on recycled paper